LYLE'S GOLDEN SYRUP©

30 best loved recipes

CONTENTS

10

38

28

36

32

44

16

42

30

LYLE'S GOLDEN SYRUP© & APRICOT FLAPJACKS

30 MINUTES PREPARATION - 25 MINUTES COOKING

MAKES 12

175g butter
100g demerara sugar
60ml LYLE'S GOLDEN SYRUP©
275g rolled oats
50g dried apricots, chopped
2tbsp pumpkin seeds
2tbsp sunflower seeds

1- Preheat the oven to 180ºC/350ºF/Gas mark 4. Grease and line the base of a 20cm square cake tin with baking paper.
2- Add the butter, sugar and LYLE'S GOLDEN SYRUP© to a pan and heat gently until the butter has melted and the sugar has dissolved. Remove from the heat and stir in the oats, seeds and chopped apricots.
3- Press the mixture into the prepared tin, pressing down firmly with the back of a spoon. Bake for 20-25 minutes until golden brown around the edges.
4- Allow to cool in the tin for 10 minutes before cutting into 12 squares. Leave to cool completely.

BAKED APPLES WITH LYLE'S GOLDEN SYRUP©

20 MINUTES PREPARATION - 20 MINUTES COOKING

SERVES 8

8 sweet apples
150g sultanas
4tbsp LYLE'S GOLDEN
SYRUP©
2tbsp butter

1- Preheat the oven to 220°C/425°F/Gas mark 7.
2- Core the apples and place them in a greased baking tin.
3- Stir the sultanas into the LYLE'S GOLDEN SYRUP© and fill the apple centres with the mixture. Drizzle a little LYLE'S GOLDEN SYRUP© over the outside of the apples.
4- Dot the top of the apples with butter.
5- Bake for 20 minutes, or until the apples have softened, basting them with the syrup mixture at regular intervals during the cooking time.
6- Serve immediately with cream or ice cream.

BANANA SMOOTHIE

3 MINUTES PREPARATION

SERVES 3

4 bananas
60ml orange juice
3 scoops vanilla ice cream
2tbsp LYLE'S GOLDEN SYRUP©
3tbsp plain yoghurt

1- Cut the bananas into small pieces and put in a blender. Add all the remaining ingredients.
2- Blend on full power for 20 seconds.
3- Serve immediately.

BBQ STICKY RIBS

25 MINUTES PREPARATION - 12 MINUTES COOKING

SERVES 2

FOR THE RIBS

1 x 6-rib pork rack

1 sprig fresh rosemary

1 sprig fresh thyme

1 garlic clove, unpeeled

FOR THE GLAZE

1tbsp LYLE'S GOLDEN SYRUP©

2tbsp tomato ketchup

1tbsp soy sauce

1tbsp soft brown sugar

1- Preheat the oven to 200°C/400°F/Gas mark 6.

2- Place the ribs in a large saucepan and cover with boiling water. Add the rosemary, thyme and unpeeled garlic clove and bring to the boil. Boil for 10 minutes, then drain and discard the water and herbs.

3- For the glaze, place the LYLE'S GOLDEN SYRUP©, ketchup, soy sauce and sugar into a small pan and simmer for 3-4 minutes or until reduced and sticky.

4- Place the blanched ribs on a baking sheet and brush with the glaze.

5- Place in the oven and cook for 10-12 minutes, or until the pork is completely cooked through.

6- Transfer the ribs to a serving dish and brush with any leftover glaze before serving.

FRUIT BRANDY SNAP BASKETS

40 MINUTES PREPARATION - 6 MINUTES COOKING

SERVES 6

FOR THE BRANDY SNAP BASKETS

110g sugar

110g butter

110ml LYLE'S GOLDEN SYRUP©

110g flour, sieved

Juice of 1 lemon

Pinch of ground ginger

1 orange

FOR THE FRUIT FILLING

200g raspberries

200g nectarines

Juice of 1 lemon

50g sugar

Whipping cream for serving

1- Make a quick syrup by melting 50g of sugar and the juice of one lemon with 2-3 tbsp of water over a medium heat. When the sugar has melted, put the syrup to one side and leave to cool. Once cool, pour the syrup over the raspberries and nectarines and leave to rest for at least an hour.

2- To make the brandy snap baskets, preheat the oven to 190°C/375°F/Gas mark 5. Line a large baking tray with greaseproof paper.

3- Melt the sugar, butter and LYLE'S GOLDEN SYRUP© together. Remove from the heat and add the flour.

4- Add the ginger and lemon juice. Place a teaspoonful of the mixture onto a baking sheet, leaving room for the mixture to spread. You may need to make two batches. Bake for around five or six minutes or until golden brown.

5- Remove from the oven and when cool enough to handle but still warm and pliable, scoop each biscuit up with a knife and lightly press around an orange, fluting the edges with your fingers before placing on a cold baking tray and pressing down firmly to create a steady base. Place int the fridge to set completely.

6- To serve, place the brandy snap baskets on plates, fill with the fruit and top with a blob of whipped cream.

BUTTERSCOTCH ICE CREAM SAUCE

20 MINUTES PREPARATION

SERVES 2

10g butter
25g soft light
brown sugar
60ml LYLE'S GOLDEN
SYRUP©
30ml double cream

1- Place butter, sugar, LYLE'S GOLDEN SYRUP© and cream in a saucepan.
2- Heat gently until the butter has melted and the sugar has dissolved, then continue to cook on a very low heat for a further 3-4 minutes, stirring continuously.
3- Pour onto your favourite ice cream and serve!

CARAMEL CHOCOLATE SHORTCAKE

25 MINUTES PREPARATION - 30 MINUTES COOKING

MAKES 12

FOR THE BASE

125g butter

50g caster sugar

175g plain flour, sieved

FOR THE FILLING

125g butter

50g caster sugar

2tbsp LYLE'S GOLDEN SYRUP©

150ml condensed milk

FOR THE TOPPING

150g dark chocolate

1- Preheat the oven to 180°C/350°F/Gas mark 4. Cream together butter and sugar for the base until light and fluffy. Add the flour and stir until the ingredients are thoroughly mixed. Knead until smooth.

2- Press this dough evenly into a 20cm square tin and prick the surface using a fork. Bake for 25-30 minutes, remove from the oven and leave to cool in the tin.

3- Meanwhile, place the filling ingredients into a saucepan and stir until the sugar has dissolved. Bring to the boil slowly, then cook, stirring continuously for 5-7 minutes. Cool slightly, then pour over the biscuit and leave to set.

4- For the topping, melt dark chocolate in a glass bowl over a pan of simmering water and spread over the caramel. Leave in the fridge to set and then cut into 12 squares with a sharp knife.

LYLE'S GOLDEN SYRUP© **CARROT CAKE**

30 MINUTES PREPARATION - I HOUR COOKING

SERVES I2

2 carrots

150g self-raising flour

75g plain flour

1tsp bicarbonate of soda

½tsp ground cinnamon

80g brown sugar

185ml vegetable oil

125ml LYLE'S GOLDEN SYRUP©

3 eggs

1tsp vanilla essence

Butter for greasing

FOR THE ICING

150g cream cheese

80g icing sugar

½tsp vanilla essence

I- Preheat the oven to 170ºC/325ºF/Gas mark 3.

2- Grease a loaf tin with butter and line with greaseproof paper. Peel and grate the carrots and set them aside.

3- Sieve the flours and bicarbonate of soda into a bowl and add the cinnamon.

4- In a separate bowl, combine the brown sugar, vegetable oil, LYLE'S GOLDEN SYRUP©, eggs and vanilla essence and use a balloon whisk to mix thoroughly.

5- Pour the syrup mixture into the dry ingredients and use a wooden spoon to gently combine. Stir in the grated carrot.

6- Pour the mixture into the cake tin and bake for one hour. Set aside for five minutes before turning out onto a wire rack to cool completely.

7- For the icing, combine the cream cheese, icing sugar and vanilla in a bowl using a wooden spoon.

8- Spread the icing over the cake and store in an airtight tin.

STICKY SOY CHICKEN WINGS

5 MINUTES PREPARATION - 40 MINUTES COOKING

SERVES 4

175ml soy sauce

125ml LYLE'S GOLDEN SYRUP©

2tsp sesame oil

½tsp fresh ginger, finely grated

Cracked black pepper

900g chicken wings

2 spring onions, finely chopped

1 lemon, cut into wedges

1- Preheat the oven to 180°C/350°F/Gas mark 4 and line a baking tray with greaseproof paper.

2- Combine the soy sauce, LYLE'S GOLDEN SYRUP©, sesame oil, grated ginger and a generous amount of black pepper in a large bowl. Add the chicken and toss to coat evenly.

3- Drain the chicken from the marinade. Place on the prepared tray and bake for 40 minutes or until golden brown and cooked through. Baste the wings halfway through the cooking time with the marinade.

4- Serve topped with spring onions and lemon wedges.

CHOCOLATE CORNFLAKE CAKES

15 MINUTES PREPARATION - 5 MINUTES COOKING - 45 MINUTES REFRIGERATION

MAKES 12-15

50g butter
100g dark chocolate
3tbsp LYLE'S GOLDEN SYRUP©
80g cornflakes
Paper cases

1- Break up the chocolate into small pieces and add it to a pan with butter and LYLE'S GOLDEN SYRUP©. Slowly melt the ingredients over a low heat, stirring continuously. When the mixture is thoroughly melted, gently stir in the cornflakes.
2- Arrange your paper cases on a baking tray. Fill each with a heaped tablespoon full of the mixture. Leave in the fridge to set for at least an hour.

LYLE'S GOLDEN SYRUP© CHOCOLATE ICING

20 MINUTES PREPARATION

MAKES ENOUGH TO DECORATE 12 SMALL FAIRY CAKES

100g plain chocolate, finely chopped

1tbsp LYLE'S GOLDEN SYRUP©

25g unsalted butter at room temperature

1- Melt the chocolate in a glass bowl over a pan of simmering water.

2- When the chocolate is thoroughly melted, add the LYLE'S GOLDEN SYRUP© and the butter. Combine thoroughly and remove from the heat. Leave to cool, stirring occasionally until the mixture reaches the right consistency for soft icing. If it thickens up too much, gently warm it through again.

3- Use an icing bag with a large nozzle to pipe the icing onto each fairy cake.

FROZEN BERRY YOGHURT

10 MINUTES PREPARATION

SERVES 4

500g mixed frozen berries
4tbsp LYLE'S GOLDEN
SYRUP©
500g natural yoghurt
Fresh mint
Fresh strawberries to
decorate

1- Pour the LYLE'S GOLDEN SYRUP© into four sundae glasses.
2- Put the yoghurt into a food processor, add the frozen berries and blend until thoroughly mixed. Add the fresh mint and blend again.
3- Spoon the mixture into the sundae glasses and top with fresh strawberries.

EASY FRUITCAKE

10 MINUTES PREPARATION - 1½ HOURS COOKING

MAKES ONE LARGE CAKE

225g self-raising flour

¼tsp salt

175g unsalted butter, at room temperature

175g muscovado sugar

175g raisins

175g sultanas

50g chopped dried fruit peel

50g glacé cherries, halved or quartered

½tsp ground ginger

½tsp ground cinnamon

3 medium eggs, lightly beaten

2tbsp LYLE'S GOLDEN SYRUP©

3tbsp brandy

3tbsp milk

1- Preheat the oven to 160°C/325°F/Gas mark 3.

2- Grease and line a 18.5 x 11.5 x 9cm loaf tin.

3- Sieve the flour and salt into a bowl. In a separate bowl, cream the sugar and the butter until soft and fluffy. Add the eggs a little at a time, followed by a tablespoon of the flour mixture and beat to mix thoroughly.

4- Add the rest of the flour and the remaining dry ingredients. Beat well. Add LYLE'S GOLDEN SYRUP© and then the dried fruit. Beat with a wooden spoon to distribute the fruit as evenly as possible.

5- Add the brandy and milk. The mixture should just drop from a spoon, but if it seems a little dry add another tablespoon or more of brandy.

6- Spoon the mixture into the prepared tin and bake for one and a half hours or until a skewer inserted into the centre of the cake comes out clean. Cool in the tin for about 15-20 minutes on a wire rack. Remove from the tin and leave to fully cool.

LYLE'S GOLDEN SYRUP© **GINGERBREAD MEN**

13 MINUTES PREPARATION - 30 MINUTES REFRIGERATION - 10 MINUTES COOKING

MAKES ABOUT 22

125g unsalted butter, softened

85g brown sugar

175ml LYLE'S GOLDEN SYRUP©

375g plain flour

2tsp ground ginger

1tsp bicarbonate of soda

1- Preheat the oven to 190ºC/375ºF/Gas mark 5. Put the butter and sugar in a bowl and beat for 10-12 minutes until light and creamy.

2- Add the LYLE'S GOLDEN SYRUP©, flour, bicarbonate of soda and ginger and beat until smooth. Refrigerate for 30 minutes.

3- Roll out the dough between sheets of non-stick baking paper to around 4mm thick. Use small gingerbread man cutters to cut out shapes in the dough. Re-roll any leftover dough until you have made all the gingerbread men you can!

4- Place on lined baking trays and bake for 8-10 minutes until golden.

LYLE'S GOLDEN SYRUP© **CUSTARD**

25 MINUTES PREPARATION

SERVES 2

300ml single cream

250ml milk

3 egg yolks

80ml **LYLE'S GOLDEN SYRUP**©

1- Combine the cream and milk in a small saucepan and bring just to the boil over a medium heat.

2- Whisk the egg yolks and LYLE'S GOLDEN SYRUP© together in a bowl until pale. Gradually stir in the hot milk mixture.

3- Transfer to a clean saucepan and stir continuously with a whisk over a low heat for 10-15 minutes or until the custard thickens enough to coat the back of a wooden spoon. Do not overheat.

4- Remove from the heat and strain into a clean jug or bowl. Drizzle a swirl of LYLE'S GOLDEN SYRUP© over the top of the custard and serve immediately.

LYLE'S GOLDEN SYRUP© **CAKE**

30 MINUTES PREPARATION · 50 MINUTES COOKING

SERVES 8

225g butter

225g light muscovado sugar

450ml LYLE'S GOLDEN SYRUP©

450g self-raising flour

2 large eggs

300ml whole milk

4tbsp LYLE'S GOLDEN SYRUP© for pouring

1- Preheat the oven to 160ºC/325ºF/Gas mark 3. Grease a 30cm cake tin and line with greaseproof paper.

2- Place the butter, LYLE'S GOLDEN SYRUP© and sugar into a large pan and heat gently until the ingredients are just melted together, stirring occasionally. Remove the pan from the hob and leave to cool for 10 minutes.

3- Beat the eggs with the milk. Add the flour and milk/egg mixture to the cooled syrup mixture in the pan and beat steadily with a wooden spoon until smooth and lump-free. Pour the mixture into the tin.

4- Bake for around 50 minutes. The cake should be well risen and springy but still very moist. Leave to cool for a few minutes, then pierce the cake all over with a skewer and spoon the extra LYLE'S GOLDEN SYRUP© over the top. Leave to cool completely in the tin.

LYLE'S GOLDEN SYRUP© **SALAD DRESSING**

SERVES 4-6

2tbsp LYLE'S GOLDEN
SYRUP©
200ml extra virgin olive oil
1tbsp white wine vinegar
1tsp Dijon mustard

1 - Mix the olive oil with LYLE'S GOLDEN SYRUP©, vinegar and
mustard and stir well. Store in an airtight bottle or jar.

LYLE'S GOLDEN SYRUP© **GRANOLA**

10 MINUTES PREPARATION - 25 MINUTES COOKING

Ⓝ

MAKES 15 BARS

2tbsp vegetable oil

150ml LYLE'S GOLDEN SYRUP©

1tsp vanilla extract

200g almonds

200g pecans

200g hazelnuts

250g rolled oats

Cinnamon to taste

1- Heat the oven to 150°C/300°F/Gas mark 2.

2- Mix the oil, LYLE'S GOLDEN SYRUP© and vanilla in a large bowl. Add all of the remaining ingredients and mix well.

3- Tip the granola onto a greased baking tray and spread out evenly. Bake for 25 minutes.

4- Once cooked, remove from the oven, cool, and store in an airtight container.

GOLDEN GREEK YOGHURT

10 MINUTES PREPARATION

(N)

SERVES 4

450g Greek yoghurt

4tbsp LYLE'S GOLDEN SYRUP©

100g pistachios, chopped

1- Pour a layer of LYLE'S GOLDEN SYRUP© into four serving dishes, then layer Greek yoghurt with chopped pistachios and a drizzle of LYLE'S GOLDEN SYRUP© until all the ingredients are used up.

2- Top with more chopped pistachios before serving.

GOLDEN HONEYCOMB

10 MINUTES PREPARATION - 10 MINUTES COOKING

SERVES 10

4tbsp LYLE'S GOLDEN SYRUP©

1tbsp water

200g caster sugar

3tsp bicarbonate of soda

1 - Grease and line a 20cm square cake tin.

2 - In a large pan, heat the LYLE'S GOLDEN SYRUP© and sugar together, bringing to the boil and then simmering on a low heat for 5-10 minutes. Test the syrup by dropping a little into cold water. If it becomes brittle it's ready!

3 - Remove the pan from the heat and add the bicarbonate of soda. Mix it in quickly as the mixture will foam up instantly.

4 - Pour immediately into the cake tin. Leave to set at room temperature and then break into bite size chunks.

LYLE'S GOLDEN SYRUP© **MOJITOS**

5 MINUTES PREPARATION

FOR ONE MOJITO YOU WILL NEED:

Fresh mint

1 lime

50ml white rum

Soda water

2tbsp LYLE'S GOLDEN SYRUP©

Crushed ice

1- Cut the lime into quarters and pick the mint leaves off the stems. Muddle a generous pinch of mint and three lime wedges in the bottom of a tall mojito glass or cocktail shaker. A wooden spoon or small rolling pin should do the trick!

2- When the ingredients are well pulverised, add ice to fill the glass.

3- Add two tablespoons of LYLE'S GOLDEN SYRUP©.

4- Add rum to the glass and stir or shake until fully blended.

5- Fill the remainder of the glass with soda water and garnish with a lime wedge and a mint leaf.

PEANUT BRITTLE

25 MINUTES PREPARATION - 30 MINUTES SETTING

(N)

SERVES 10

60g butter
180g sugar
1tbsp water
200ml LYLE'S GOLDEN
SYRUP©
200g salted peanuts

1- Lightly grease a baking tray.
2- Put the butter, water and sugar in a saucepan and heat slowly on a gentle heat, stirring all the time, until the butter melts.
3- Add LYLE'S GOLDEN SYRUP© and continue to heat and stir until the sugar dissolves. Boil slowly, stirring continuously. Test the syrup by dropping a little in some cold water. If it turns hard, it's ready!
4- Add the peanuts and keep heating and stirring. The peanuts will have cooled it down a little so test another drop in cold water. When it hardens in the water, it's ready.
5- Carefully pour into a baking tray and leave to harden for about 30 minutes.
6- Break with a toffee hammer or with the handle of a heavy knife.

BARBECUED THAI PRAWN SKEWERS

5 MINUTES PREPARATION - 1 HOUR REFRIGERATION - 5 MINUTES COOKING

SERVES 4 AS A STARTER

24 uncooked prawns, peeled

2tbsp coriander, chopped, plus extra to garnish

1tbsp fresh ginger, grated

1tbsp soy sauce

1tbsp LYLE'S GOLDEN SYRUP©

1 garlic clove, crushed

Zest and juice of 2 limes

1- Soak the bamboo skewers in water for one and a half hours so that they don't burn.

2- In a bowl, combine the ginger, soy sauce, LYLE'S GOLDEN SYRUP©, garlic, chopped coriander and the lime zest and juice. Place the prawns in the same bowl, cover and refrigerate until you are ready to start cooking. If possible, allow to marinate for at least one hour.

3- Thread the prawns onto the skewers and BBQ for two minutes on each side until cooked and a little blackened. Garnish with coriander and serve immediately.

LYLE'S GOLDEN SYRUP© **STEAMED PUDDING**

10 MINUTES PREPARATION - 2 HOURS COOKING

SERVES 6

1tbsp black treacle

3tbsp LYLE'S GOLDEN SYRUP©, plus 3 extra tbsp for serving

175g self-raising flour

1tsp baking powder

175g softened butter

3 large eggs

175g soft brown sugar

1- Grease a pudding basin, then measure three tablespoons of LYLE'S GOLDEN SYRUP© into it. In a mixing bowl, sieve the flour and baking powder. Add the butter, eggs, sugar and treacle.

2- Use an electric whisk to beat the mixture thoroughly. Now spoon the mixture into the basin and level the top using the back of a tablespoon. Cover the entire pudding bowl in foil. Half fill a large saucepan with water and sit the basin in the water to create a bain-marie.

3- Steam the pudding for two hours, checking the water level halfway through and topping up if necessary. To serve, loosen the pudding all the way around the bowl using a palette knife, invert it onto a warmed plate, and pour an extra three tablespoons of warmed LYLE'S GOLDEN SYRUP© over the top.

LYLE'S GOLDEN SYRUP© **TREACLE TARTS**

40 MINUTES PREPARATION - 25 MINUTES COOKING

SERVES 4

350g ready-made
shortcrust pastry

160ml LYLE'S GOLDEN
SYRUP©

1 lemon

75g fresh breadcrumbs

1 egg white

1- Preheat the oven to 200°C/400°F/Gas mark 6.

2- On a lightly floured surface, roll out three-quarters of the pastry to around 3mm thickness. Transfer it to four greased 10cm tart tins and trim off any overhang, ensuring you keep the trimmings. Place in the fridge for 20 minutes.

3- Warm the LYLE'S GOLDEN SYRUP© gently in a pan until it melts.

4- Remove the syrup from the heat and stir in the breadcrumbs and the rind of the lemon. Whip one egg white until it forms stiff peaks. While the syrup is cooling, fold in the egg white. Leave to stand for 10 minutes, then add more breadcrumbs if the mixture is too wet. Stir in 30ml of lemon juice, then spread the mixture evenly between the four tins.

5- Roll out the leftover pastry and cut it into 48 thin strips. Don't worry about being too precise! Twist the strips into spirals then arrange them into lattices over each tart.

6- Place the tarts in the oven and bake for 10 minutes. Reduce the temperature to 190°C/375°F/Gas mark 5 and bake for another 15 minutes until golden.

BBQ SAUCE

10 MINUTES PREPARATION - 20 MINUTES COOKING

MAKES I JAR

2tbsp olive oil
4 cloves garlic, finely chopped
1 onion, finely chopped
200g tomato puree
180g cider vinegar
5tbsp soy sauce
5tbsp LYLE'S GOLDEN SYRUP©
1tsp Chinese five spice powder
1tbsp mustard
5tbsp honey
Black pepper
200ml chicken stock

1- Sauté the garlic and onion in the oil until translucent and soft.
2- Add all the remaining ingredients, except the stock, and bring to the boil.
3- Reduce the heat and simmer. Little by little, pour in the stock until the sauce thickens, but keep stirring all the time.
4- Serve the sauce warm or cold. Store in an airtight jar in the fridge.

LYLE'S GOLDEN SYRUP© **AND BACON PANCAKE**

15 MINUTES PREPARATION - 5 MINUTES COOKING

SERVES 2

50g plain flour
1 egg
100ml semi-skimmed milk
25ml water
LYLE'S GOLDEN SYRUP©
Crispy bacon

1- Sift the flour into a mixing bowl. Make a well in the centre and add the egg. Add the water to the egg.
2- Slowly beat the egg and water mixture into the flour with a wooden spoon, then add the milk a little at a time, beating until you have a smooth batter.
3- Cook each pancake in a little oil until golden on both sides.
4- Serve with hot crispy bacon and drizzled with LYLE'S GOLDEN SYRUP©.

CRUMPETS WITH LYLE'S GOLDEN SYRUP©

5 MINUTES COOKING

SERVES 2

4 crumpets
Butter
LYLE'S GOLDEN SYRUP©

1- Toast your crumpets until crispy.
2- Butter them liberally and then spread with a generous helping of LYLE'S GOLDEN SYRUP©.
3- Serve immediately.

FRUITY BREAKFAST PORRIDGE

5 MINUTES COOKING

SERVES 2

100g porridge oats
700ml milk
2tbsp LYLE'S GOLDEN
SYRUP©
Fresh blackberries,
blueberries and
raspberries

1- Add the milk to the porridge oats and cook over a medium heat, stirring continuously to avoid lumps.
2- Divide the porridge into two bowls, heap with the fresh berries and drizzle each bowl with one tablespoon of LYLE'S GOLDEN SYRUP©.

DECADENT CHOCOLATE DIPPING SAUCE

Great for drizzling, dipping and dunking anything - from doughnuts to fresh pineapple.

15 MINUTES PREPARATION

100g milk chocolate

25g butter, at room temperature

25g demerara sugar

1tbsp LYLE'S GOLDEN SYRUP©

2tbsp semi-skimmed milk

1- Melt the chocolate, butter, sugar, milk and LYLE'S GOLDEN SYRUP© in a glass bowl over a pan of simmering water. Stir until thoroughly combined.

2- Serve immediately as the sauce will thicken up as it cools.

READER SERVICES

CUSTOMER SERVICE IN THE UK AND REPUBLIC OF IRELAND

How to continue your collection:
Customers can either place an order with their newsagent or receive issues on subscription.
Back issues: Either order through your newsagent or write to:
30 Best Loved Recipes, Jacklin Enterprises UK, PO Box 77, Jarrow, NE32 3YH,
enclosing payment of the cover price plus £0.50 p&p per copy.
(Republic of Ireland: cover price plus €1.00).
Subscriptions: You can have your issues sent directly to your home (postage and packing
free). For details, see insert in issue 1 or phone our Subscription Hotline on 0871 472 4240
(Monday to Friday, 9am–5pm, calls cost 10p per minute from the UK only).
Alternatively, you can write to 30 Best Loved Recipes, Jacklin Enterprises UK, PO Box 77,
Jarrow, NE32 3YH, or fax your enquiries to 0871 472 4241,
or e-mail: 30bestlovedrecipes@jacklinservice.com.
Alternatively, order online at www.bestlovedrecipes.co.uk

This book has created by Hachette Partworks with the cooperation of
TATE AND LYLE
Published by Hachette Partworks Ltd,
Jordan House, 47 Brunswick Place, London, N1 6EB.
Photography: Jess Esposito   **Styling & Food Preparation:** Helen Rance

Distributed in the UK and Republic of Ireland by Marketforce.
© 2013 Hachette Partworks Ltd
Printed in Spain.
ISSN 2049-9302

 Recipes with this symbol contain nuts